Doing The
WHITE PASS

Howard Clifford

The story of the White Pass
& Yukon Route and the
Klondike Gold Rush

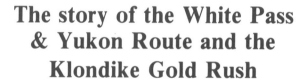

Sourdough Enterprises
16401 3rd Ave. S.W.
Seattle, WA., 98166

ISBN — 0-911803-04-1

Library of Congress Catalog Card No. 82-062466

First Printing 1983

Second Printing 1988

Thanks to the White Pass & Yukon Route for permission to use art work of locomotive No. 73 on the cover.

Published by
Sourdough Enterprises
16401 3rd Ave. S.W.
Seattle, WA., 98166

Foreword

"The railroad that was impossible to build," was nearly so, except for the expertise of Mike Heney, colorful Canadian construction man who delighted in taking on "impossible" challenges.

This book is the story of the building of that railroad, and the events leading up to the actual start of construction, such as the imagination of Captain William Moore, the discovery of gold in the Klondike and the tortures of the "Dead Horse Trail."

It is also the story of the White Pass and Yukon Route, the 110-mile, narrow gauge railroad, probably the most scenic railroad in the world.

This book could not have been written without the help of dozens of others who went out of their way making it possible to put together the research, the story material and the photographs that have made it all possible. People such as Diane Johnston and Marion Ridge of the Yukon Archives; Bob Monroe and Dennis Anderson of the University of Washington Library, Northwest Collection; Randolph J. and the late Joseph J. Smith, grandsons of the infamous Jefferson Randolph "Soapy" Smith; the many Skagway residents who have witnessed history in the making, such as Edna and George Rapuzzi, Georgette and Jack Kirmse, Cy Coyne, Barbara Kalen of Dedman's Photo Shop; Bill Feero; Anna and J.D. True; Frank Downey, formerly with the WP&YR; and many others.

Also a big special thanks to Steve Hites, a railroad buff and historian par excellence, who provided much in the way of historical material as well as reading copy and proofs, seeking out errors and would-be mistakes. Thanks too, to the White Pass & Yukon Route for making it possible for us to use art work of steam locomotive No. 73 on our cover. It is much appreciated.

To all—plus anyone I might have overlooked—a great big Thank You.

Howard Clifford
January 1983

Contents

Chapter I

Discovery In The Yukon

Dreams of a 65-year old sea captain, who had gone through close to a dozen gold rushes and who had made and lost several fortunes, foretold the construction of the White Pass & Yukon Route a decade before the discovery of gold in the Yukon.

During the summer of 1887 Captain William (Billy) Moore was hired by a Canadian survey party, headed by William Ogilvie, to find a new route from sea level to the Upper Yukon—a route that could be reached from the placid waters of Tiaya Inlet on Lynn Canal.

At that time entry into the Upper Yukon Valley was via the Chilkoot Pass, a precipitous and rugged route that taxed the strength of the best of men. Captain Moore had traveled the area over a period of years and had heard rumors of such a route, more than 600 feet less in altitude than the Chilkoot.

He was determined to test the feasibility of a new route and so while the main Ogilvie party took the old trail through Dyea,

1

an Indian village centered around the Healy and Wilson Trading Post and supplier to most of those going over the pass, Capt. Moore started up the Skagway (Skaguay) River, accompanied by his Indian friend, Skookum Jim Mason, who was to play an even more important role in the Klondike gold rush a decade later.

Traveling where there was no trail or evidence of previous travel, over precarious switchbacks, up almost vertical hillsides and rugged canyons, Capt. Moore and his companion reached the headwaters of the Yukon several days after the main Ogilvie party—but over an entirely new and lower pass. Capt. Moore was most enthusiastic over the new route and in accepting the old sea captain's report that it was passable and showed promise of easing the trek to the Yukon, Ogilvie named White Pass after Thomas White, Canadian Minister of the Interior.

Capt. Moore remained with the Ogilvie party for another two months and the Canadian explorer later reported that every night the craggy old sea captain dreamed of another great gold rush, pictured tons of yellow dust yet to be discovered in the Yukon Valley, and dreamed of the White Pass eventually reverberating with the rumble of railway trains carrying tons of supplies in and precious gold out, and that Skagway Bay would be the entry point.

So enthusiastic was Capt. Moore over his new-found route that he and his son Ben left the Ogilvie party and on October 20, 1887 settled at the present site of Skagway, pitching a tent on a small knoll and staking claim to a 160-acre townsite. He told his son, "I fully expect before many years to see a pack train through this pass, followed by a wagon road, and I would not be at all surprised to see a railroad through to the lakes."

The pair started working on cribbing for a wharf near the east side of the bay at the foot of a high steep rocky bluff. This became the basis of the steamship wharf along the bluff used by today's cruise ships.

They also built a log cabin, which still stands at its original site and is part of the present-day Klondike Gold Rush National Historical Park along with Capt. Moore's house, the first frame building to be constructed in Skagway. It was later moved to the present site beside the original cabin.

Despite lack of stable financial backing—perhaps due to his

If it had not been for these two there probably would not have been a Skagway, a White Pass & Yukon railroad, or a Klondike gold rush. At the left is Skookum Jim Mason, trapper, guide and prospector, who was with Captain Billy Moore (right) when he explored the White Pass. A decade later Mason discovered gold in the Klondike. Capt. Moore was the first white man to go through the pass, build a trail to the summit and was the first settler in Skagway.

Clifford collection

frightful financial history—Capt. Moore continued his development work and by the summer of 1897 had cleared and blazed a trail with bridges all the way to the lakes, enlarged his wharf and built a sawmill.

In the meantime, a decade after Capt. Moore's dream of the discovery of gold in the Yukon, that dream came true.

On August 17, 1896, Capt. Moore's friend Skookum Jim, accompanied by his nephew Tagish Charlie and his brother-in-law George Carmack, was exploring and cutting wood in the Yukon. He stopped for a drink of water from Rabbit Creek, discovering unheard of quantities of gold. Some reports state that a fourth person, believed to be Kate Carmack, George's wife and Jim's sister, was also present. Patsy Henderson, the younger brother of Tagish Charlie and nephew of Skookum

3

Jim, later claimed to have been present, but was too young to get any credit in the discovery.

Because of the fact that an Indian could not file for a discovery claim, it was decided that Carmack (the only white person in the party) would file as the discoverer and split the claim with Skookum Jim. Carmack also filed for himself and his two partners. (Under Canadian law, no more than one claim could be staked in any mining district by anyone except the discoverer, who was allowed a double claim.)

The filing resulted in a stampede by most of the approximately 1,700 prospectors in the Yukon at the time and by August 31 all of Bonanza Creek (as Rabbit Creek became known) was staked with every claim from No. 1 through No. 40 being worth at least half a million (with gold at $20 an ounce) and a good number many times that amount.

Capt. Billy Moore's log cabin was the first building in Skagway and still stands on the little knoll near a stream where it was built. It is part of the Klondike National Historical Park.

Clifford photo

APPLICATION AND AFFIDAVIT ~~OF DISCOVERY OF QUARTZ~~ *for Placer* MINE.

I, *G. W. Carmack*
of *Forty-Mile*
hereby apply, under the Dominion Lands Mining Regulations, for a mining location in

a Creek known as Bonanza Creek flowing into Klondike River.

Discovery claim on Bonanza Creek.

for the purpose of mining for *Gold*
and I hereby solemnly swear :—

1. That I have discovered therein a deposit of *Gold*.

2. That I was, to the best of my knowledge and belief, the first discoverer of the said deposit.

3. That I am unaware that the land is other than vacant Dominion land.

4. That I did, on the *17th* day of *August* 1896, mark out on the ground, in accordance in every particular with the provisions of ~~sub-section (a) of section four of~~ the said Mining Regulations, the location for which I make this application; and that in so doing I did not encroach on any mining location previously laid out by any other person.

5. That the said mining location contains, as nearly as I could measure or estimate, an area of ....
acres, and that the description and (sketch, if any) of this date hereto attached, signed by ...., set forth in detail, to the best of .... knowledge and ability, its position, form and dimensions.

6. That I make this application in good faith to acquire the land for the sole purpose of mining to be prosecuted by myself or by myself and associates, or by my assigns.

Sworn before me at *H. Constantine*
this *22d* day of *September*
1896 *Constantine*
a commissioner   } *G. W. Carmack*

Note—In case of abandoned ground it may be necessary to omit No. 3.

Form No. 100.

George Carmack's gold claim filing for the discovery claim on Bonanza Creek (Rabbit Creek), which started the stampede to the Klondike.

Clifford collection

The cabin in the left foreground (arrow) marks the site where Skookum Jim made the first discovery of gold on Bonanza Creek (Rabbit Creek) which started the Klondike gold rush. Gold Hill is on the right with the mouth of Eldorado Creek just behind Gold Hill.

University of Washington, Hegg collection

Had it not been for the fact that he hated Indians and went out of his way on at least two occasions to insult those with Carmack, Robert Henderson, a well-known and respected Canadian who had prospected in the Yukon for many years, might have been in on the riches. Henderson had made a modest find on nearby Gold Bottom Creek and told Carmack about it. When Carmack asked about filing a claim there, Henderson remarked, "It's all right for you, George, but I don't want any damn Siwashes staking a claim there."

Later when the Carmack party had run out of food (and tobacco, so important to the Indians) Henderson refused to sell any tobacco to Carmack's friends although he did supply food. Thus, while Henderson was only over the next ridge from the Carmack party when the discovery was made, they did not follow the miner's code and notify him so he too could share in the riches before "outsiders" grabbed off the better claims. By the time Henderson learned of the find, all the good claims were gone.

Tents of Dawson City in 1898, prior to the construction of"permanent" wooden buildings. During the height of the Klondike rush Dawson became a city of 40,000 persons.

Yukon Archives, Vancouver Public Library collection

One who did benefit from the discovery, but in a different way, was Joe Ladue, a prosperous trader at Sixty Mile. He closed his trading post, joined the stampede and staked out a townsite on the low land at the confluence of the Klondike and Yukon Rivers, some three miles from Bonanza Creek. He named it Dawson City, after George M. Dawson, a Canadian government geologist.

Ladue floated in a sawmill and by April 1897 there were 1,500 people in two ragged tent cities. One was Dawson City and the other across the Klondike River became Klondike City—also known as Lousetown and White Chapel.

Lots were selling for $12,000 each and eventually went as high as $40,000 as Dawson City grew to 40,000 persons, the largest city east of Chicago and north of San Francisco. The city was known as the "Paris of the North" and became the

7

capital of the Yukon and remained so until 1953 when the territorial government was moved to Whitehorse.

Wide-open gambling prevailed and as much as $20,000 could be lost in one spin of the roulette wheel, $5,000 at stud poker or $1,000 at the throw of the dice. Dance hall queens and Bonanza kings were in their heyday.

Dawson City went through two disasterous fires—blamed on dance hall girls—and was rebuilt each time, although after the second blaze, which destroyed more than 100 buildings and did damage of more than $1,000,000, the city was never the same.

In June 1900 news arrived that gold had been struck on the beaches of Nome. There was another stampede, but this time away from the Yukon. The Klondike gold rush was over as quickly as it began.

Syndicates and banks, however, still saw the value of the untouched gold of the Yukon. A narrow gauge railroad, the Klondike Mines Railway and Stage Co., was built from

This plaque marks the site of the original discovery of gold on Rabbit Creek, later known as Bonanza Creek, resulting in the Klondike stampede, the greatest gold rush in history.

Clifford photo

Dawson City at the height of the gold rush as seen from across the Klondike River. Known as the "Paris of the North," Dawson City became the largest city west of Chicago and north of San Francisco.
University of Washington, Hegg collection.

Front Street, Dawson City, during the height of the gold rush. Dawson City became a booming city of 40,000 persons.
Clifford collection

Klondike City to the summit of Dome Mountain, a distance of 31 miles, to haul in heavy equipment and to supply the soon-to-be-built gold dredges. Work started in July 1906 with E. C. Hawkins, the White Pass & Yukon engineer, playing an important role in the construction.

The railroad operated until July 1914 when it was abandoned and later the right-of-way was turned over to the government for construction of a highway from Six Below to Bonanza. That highway is still in use today.

Three of the four locomotives used by the KM were obtained from the White Pass and are on display at Minto Park in Dawson City, along with a little saddle-tanker which was used to haul coal for the Northern Light, Power, Coal and Transportation Co., which supplied Dawson City with coal and electricity. A fourth Klondike Mines locomotive was requisitioned by the U. S. Army for the White Pass & Yukon for wartime use during World War II.

Chapter II

A Ton Of Gold

When the ice went out on the Yukon in the spring of 1897 the Portus B. Weare and the Alice started on a 1,700-mile voyage to the sea with a group of happy prospectors and their suitcases of gold, boxes of gold, packing cases of gold and belts and pokes of gold—along with jam jars, medicine bottles and tomato cans, all full of gold.

Eighty prospectors with three tons of gold boarded the S.S. Excelsior, the S.S. Portland and the S.S. Humboldt at St. Michael headed for San Francisco, Seattle and San Diego. Although the Excelsior arrived in San Francisco first, it was the landing of the Portland in Seattle with its "ton of gold" that started the greatest gold rush in history.

The ship was met off Port Townsend by Berish Brown, an energetic reporter from the Seattle Post Intelligencer, who filed

11

Stampeders unloaded their goods from the steamers on barges and scows at Skagway and then teamsters hauled them to shore during the early days of the Klondike stampede. Pilings for wharves under construction can be seen in the background. Later these same teamsters put their wagons to good use over the Brackett Road to the summit of White Pass.

Washington State Historical Society

the story on the Associated Press wire. This was followed up by the work of one, Erastus Brainard, a former east coast newspaper editor who considered himself a "statesman of the press." In other words, one of the cleverest of publicity men ever in the employ of the Seattle Chamber of Commerce. For weeks not a day, hour, and some say minute went by without an AP story by Brainard on the gold rush and the Klondike, all with a Seattle dateline

The time was right for the lunacy that followed. The country was in the throes of a depression, the world was at peace, and there was nothing to rival the Klondike for the world's attention. That was the start of Seattle becoming the "Gateway to Alaska."

Soon stampeders were pouring ashore at Skagway like a conquering horde, paying little attention to the protesting

Capt. Moore. It was as if he was one of the trees they slashed down to make room for their tents and shacks. They heaped their supplies and goods on the beach and tethered their animals in the forest. They hacked, burned and gouged away at the beautiful wooded delta and a rough semblace of town emerged. Skagway was born.

One of those who led the takeover was Frank Reid, an ex-school teacher and Indian fighter, who had been accused of inciting Indian warfare in Oregon and who was tried for killing an unarmed man and acquitted on the grounds of "self-defense." The argonauts named him to survey the town.

Reid soon determined that Capt. Moore's homestead was athwart one of the main streets of the town and ordered its removal or destruction despite Capt. Moore's protestations and the fact that the old sea dog had previously laid out and filed on a townsite for Skagway.

Skagway "officials" move Captain Billy Moore's residence from its original site on October 15, 1898 after Surveyor Frank Reid determined it was athwart one of the main streets in town, despite a previous platting of the City of Skagway by Captain Moore.

Yukon Archives

Not only did Reid and his cohorts bodily remove Billy Moore's home, but they sold the choice lots in town at exorbitant prices to the stampeders, not once, but many times over. As soon as one purchaser left for the gold fields his property was sold to another who had just arrived in town.

Capt. Moore eventually took his case to the United States District Court for redress, and then as now, the courts moved slowly. Four years later, however, the court decided in Capt. Moore's favor and awarded him 25 percent of the assessed valuation of the improvements made on his and his son's 160-acre homestead. While awaiting action of the court Capt. Moore, seeing that there was money to be made in Skagway, relocated and extended his wharf out across the tidal flat to deep water, facilitating the landing of the hundreds of ships that were yet to come.

Packers with horses and dogs make their way through the wooded area on the lower reaches of the Skagway (White Pass) Trail. The narrow trail caused problems as those hauling loads to the summit tried to pass the on-coming down trail traffic.

Clifford collection

Captain Billy Moore's sawmill earned the old sea dog a small fortune as he turned out lumber for the construction of Skagway. The town in the early days was a mixture of tents and wooden buildings.

Clifford collection

When word was received on the West Coast that a pack trail was open across the White Pass, animals of every sort were shipped to Skagway to be used on the trail as pack animals, providing cheaper, easier and quicker transportatin over the coast mountains to the lakes.

Canadian authorities would not allow the argonauts to cross the border unless they had supplies enough to last a year, roughly 1,100 pounds. Getting these supplies over the passes to the headwaters of the Yukon at Lake Bennett was the most trying part of the trip to the Klondike. Once at the lakes, boat building was the main occupation.

With Klondike traffic growing heavier by the day, improvements in transportation over the original trail as set up by Capt. Moore became an item of top priority.

The Chilkoot Pass was also a popular route to the interior with its various tramways, which eventually joined together under an agreement that gave the Chilkoot an edge. This advantage, however, was eliminated by the disasterous slide above Sheep Camp on April 3, 1898, which killed scores of prospectors.

THE GOLD RUSH TRAIL

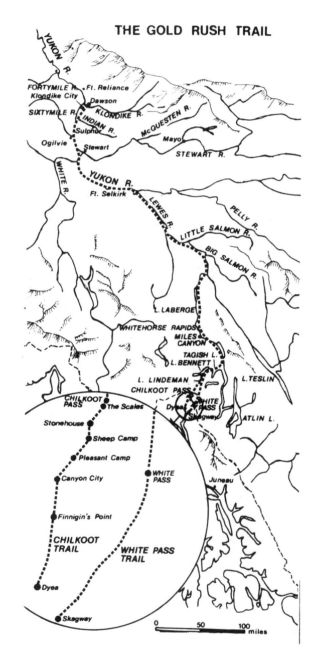

YUKON R.

FORTYMILE R. • Ft. Reliance
Klondike City
SIXTYMILE R. Dawson
KLONDIKE R.
INDIAN R.
Sulphur McQUESTEN R.
Ogilvie Mayo
Stewart STEWART R.

WHITE R.
YUKON R.
Ft. Selkirk
LEWES R.
PELLY R.
LITTLE SALMON R.
BIG SALMON R.

L. LABERGE
WHITEHORSE RAPIDS
MILES CANYON
TAGISH L.
L. BENNETT
L. TESLIN
L. LINDEMAN
CHILKOOT PASS
CHILKOOT PASS
The Scales WHITE PASS
Stonehouse Dyea Skagway ATLIN L.
Sheep Camp
Pleasant Camp
Canyon City WHITE PASS Juneau
Finnigin's Point
CHILKOOT TRAIL
WHITE PASS TRAIL
Dyea
Skagway

0   50   100 miles

Map Courtesy Parks Canada

16

The steep, treacherous "Golden Stairs" on the Chilkoot Pass caught the fancy of the early day news media and brought attention to the Chilkoot route while overlooking the lower, and less spectacular White Pass route. Note tramway towers at the right, which those who could afford it used to transport their goods to the top.

Clifford collection

As early as August 1897 traffic on the White Pass Trail was moving at a snail's pace due to congestion of some 2,000 adventurers who were strung out along the trail with much of their gear in a sorry condition or practically worthless.

Once the snows came and the river froze in the late autumn of 1897 pack horses and mules could be used out of Skagway, giving the White Pass route an advantage. Horses could carry 250 pounds besides their feed between Skagway and Lake Bennett, taking four days to make the journey. Some of the packers who had 40 to 50 horses on the trail were able to net $1,000 a day on an investment of $2,000 to $3,000.

Such was the haste to get across the pass under the terrible conditions of the trail that horses by the hundreds broke their legs on the boulder-strewn stretches and had to be destroyed. They worked under trying conditions with little or no food. By September 1897 veteran horseman Major J. M. Walsh of the North West Mounted Police, enroute to the Klondike as Commissioner of the Yukon, said:

"Such a scene of havoc and destruction ... can scarcely be imagined. Thousands of pack horses lie dead along the way, sometimes in bunches under the cliffs, with pack-saddles and packs where they had fallen from the rocks above, sometimes in tangled masses filling the mud holes and furnishing the only footing for more animals to follow."

Jack London, who was destined to gain fame for his novels of the North Country, crossed White Pass in the autumn of 1897 and what he saw of the trail sickened him. He wrote:

"The horses died like mosquitoes in the first frost of winter and from Skagway to Bennett they rotted in heaps. They died at the rocks, they were poisoned at the summit, they starved at the lakes, they fell off the trail ... in the river they drowned under their loads or were smashed to pieces against the boulders, they snapped their legs in the crevises and broke their backs falling backwards with their packs."

This was Dead Horse Trail. Thousands of horses died here.

Carcasses of dead horses litter the "Dead Horse Trail" over the White Pass to the lakes above. Thousands of horses lost their lives during the early days of the stampede to the Klondike.

Dedman Photo Shop

A sign along the way marks the Trail of '98 on the way to the Klondike.
The marker is along the present-day White Pass route and one may
clearly see the well-worn trail through the rugged rocky terrain.

Clifford photo

Chapter III

Brackett's Wagon Road

Though past what was considered the prime of life in others, 61-year old George A. Brackett, ex-mayor of Minneapolis, set out courageously and self-reliantly for Alaska to rehabilitate his fortunes.

By October 1897—four months after the first gold landed in Seattle—he had taken two lots, bought two cabins, and was purchasing supplies in Seattle to send to Dyea, having decided to initiate a business selling goods to the scores of prospectors journeying to the Klondike via the Chilkoot Pass.

On the way north he met Judge J. H. Acklen, a former Tennessee congressman who had an interest in building a road over the mountains to facilitate moving men and goods to the gold fields. Learning of Brackett's railroad building experiences, Acklen included him in future plans.

The two met again on a trip southward and by that time Acklen was convinced that the White Pass was more feasible than the Chilkoot for construction of such a road. He urged Brackett to join him, engineer Norman Smith and about 15 of Skagway's leading merchants, in forming the Skaguay and Yukon Transportation and Improvement Co., to build a road and eventually a railroad over White Pass.

At first reluctant on the White Pass route, Brackett was gradually caught up in the Skagway venture with some urging from an old friend, Captain Charles A. Peabody, manager of the Washington Alaska Steamship Co.

Brackett was hired as general superintendent at $500 a month, although the only money on hand was his own $3,500. It did not take Brackett long to discover that he was involved in a great deal of boom enterprise—all stock, no money.

Without waiting to secure a franchise to collect tolls, Brackett plunged into the enterprise. Work started on November 8, 1897 and even without funds Brackett and his crews completed four miles of roadway out of Skagway and opened it to traffic on November 23, 1897. By mid-December eight miles had been completed and opened. By December 30 Brackett was broke. He returned to Minnesota and starting

Downtown Skagway in May 1898, before the White Pass & Yukon railroad tracks were laid down the center of Broadway. Note the wagons, many of which made regular trips over the Brackett Wagon Road to the summit of White Pass.

Dedman Photo Shop

The White Pass Trail becomes a quagmire during the early fall months as thousands of stampeders make their way to the summit of White Pass. Tons of equipment is discared along the trail, left there to rot as the going got rough.

Clifford collection

with a nest-egg from the Great Northern Railroad, was able to raise additional funds from officials of the Canadian Pacific and others.

On his trip "outside" to seek funds, Brackett was befriended by one Jefferson Randolph "Soapy" Smith, who had taken up residence in Skagway the previous summer, opening Soapy Smith's Parlor and other establishments. He made frequent trips to the Pacific Northwest and the East on business and to visit his family.

Smith was a controversial figure in Skagway, a colorful and adroit confidence man—a sort of Robin Hood to many, and an outlaw to others. He did however, carry considerable weight with the tougher element in the community.

Shortly after his return to Skagway in mid-January, Brackett increased his labor force, but trouble developed as a trio of outlaws took possession of a section of the road, stating

George Brackett, kneeling center, developer of the Brackett Wagon Road to the summit of White Pass, goes over plans with some of his construction crew on one of the log bridges which spanned the many streams in the area.

National Archives

Workmen clear the right-of-way for the Brackett Wagon Road to the summit of White Pass, using the tools of the day—sledge hammers and crow bars. Work on the road started in 1897. Note the relaxed workman holding the steel chisel as the other workman is about to strike a heavy blow.

National Archives

that they had located a mineral claim. The authorities refused to help and Brackett called upon his new-found friend, Smith. Soapy rode up with some of his followers and told the outlaws that "they should be ashamed of themselves, as the highway was bringing prosperity to the country," and threatened to have his followers toss them into the Skagway River if they didn't leave.

None were about to test Smith's authority and they soon departed.

Several days later was payday on the Brackett Road. A number of the workers cashed and squandered their checks in Soapy's Parlor on Holly Street. Brackett felt sorry for those who had families and confronted Smith over the matter, stating he appreciated Smith's help in opening the road, but did not appreciate his men being "swindled" in Soapy's place.

Smith returned their funds and subsequently Brackett's employees were welcome to cash their checks at Soapy's, but were not enticed into games of chance in his Parlor.

Employing his political influence, Brackett was able to get legislation passed delegating to the Secretary of the Interior authority to grant permission to levy a toll.

Despite the fact that the road had not been completed to the summit and the bridge was not yet over the East Fork, Brackett started charging tolls of two cents a pound for freight, a dollar for each pedestrian, a dollar for each horse, mule or oxen, twenty-five cents for each sheep or dog, and $10 for each wagon, for use of the completed portion of the road. Hard-boiled freighters and packers refused to pay and destroyed the toll gates erected by Brackett.

His attempts to collect tolls for passage above White Pass City led to the "Toll Gate War."

Brackett wired an old friend in the War Department who complained to higher ups "that a rowdy element had seized the wagon road and had placed the country in a state of terror." This brought assistance from Col. Thomas Anderson and his troops at Dyea.

By mid-April the bridge was completed over the East Fork and the toll road was bringing in a modest $1,000 to $1,500 a day. This was not as much as Brackett had hoped for. Despite additional financial assistance from backers in the states and passage of the Lacey Bill extending the Homestead Act to

Alaska, thus providing for construction of wagon roads, trails and railroads, Brackett was still strapped for money and fought a continuing and losing battle with packers and freighters on payment of tolls.

The Brackett Road and the White Pass Trail in 1898 became the routes of the freighter and packer rather than the cheechako. Consequently while there are hundreds of accounts describing a trip over the Chilkoot Trail to the Klondike, there are very few detailing the crossing of White Pass. Undoubtedly the prime reason for the paucity of published accounts of such journeys across the White Pass is that the editors and readers were more impressed with photographs of the human chain climbing the "golden stairs." Stories of high adventure on the Chilkoot Trail made better copy and sold, while with the passing of the "Dead Horse Trail" there was little to spark reader interest in the less spectacular route across White Pass.

The line is long and slow as Canadian customs officers check goods and collect duties as stampeders make their way to the Klondike. Stampeders were required to have and pay duty on one year's supplies before Canadian Northwest Mounted Police would allow them to enter the country.

University of Washington, Hegg collection

Chapter IV

A Railroad Is Born

Meanwhile three Victoria businessmen, who had listened to and believed in Capt. Moore and his railroad over White Pass, obtained a charter to build a railroad over the Canadian portion of the route.

They also obtained the initial funds from Close Brothers of London, one of the largest British financial houses, with the stipulation that construction was to start by a pre-determined date. Unable to obtain additional funds or the other necessary permits resulted in default and Close Brothers gained possession of an "invisible piece of property known as a franchise."

Close Brothers, without ever having seen the country or having a representative look over the ground, decided to build the railroad themselves, providing the proper construction experts could be obtained to handle the job.

They delegated Sir Thomas Tanerede to contact knowledgeable experts and visit Skagway and the White Pass area early in 1898. He was accompanied on the trip by Samuel H. Graves of the firm's Chicago office, and Samuel L. Hawkins, a Seattle engineer.

The trio explored the White Pass and came to the conclusion that the mountains were too massive, the sheer walls of the cliffs too steep, and the grades required too great. As a result, Sir Thomas decided to advise his backers that the railroad was impossible to build.

Michael J. "Big Mike" Heney, a Canadian railroad contractor who had played an important role in the construction of the Canadian Pacific Railroad, had also explored the White Pass. Despite viewing the same obstacles that had discouraged Sir Thomas and his party, Heney was convinced that a railroad could be built to the summit and lakes, providing financing was available.

The chance meeting of Sir Thomas and Heney in the bar of the St. James Hotel, as each was awaiting ship transportation south, changed the entire picture. They spent the night in thorough discussion of the area, the problems and the like and according to local legend, when dawn broke they drank a toast to the success of the construction of a railroad over White Pass.

After the meeting of Heney and Sir Thomas the paper work necessary to organize the railroad was quickly put together. The incorporation of the Pacific & Arctic Railway and Navigation Co. on March 28, 1898 in West Virginia enabled them to obtain a charter for a right-of-way through United States government land as Congress extended the Homestead Laws, providing for the right-of-way for railroads in the District of Alaska, on May 14, 1898.

Formed at the same time was the British Columbia Yukon Railway Co., which was granted a legislative charter in British Columbia, and the British Yukon Railway Co., which was granted a charter to build and operate in the Yukon as provided by an Act of Parliament of the Dominion of Canada.

The White Pass & Yukon Route was registered on July 30, 1898 to carry out the charters and concessions of the three companies.

The first order of business was the naming of Mike Heney as contractor, Erastus C. Hawkins, chief engineer, and John

The St. James Hotel on Fourth, just off Broadway originally located at the corner of Fourth and State Streets where Mike Heney and Sir Thomas Tanerede first met and decided that they could build a railroad over the White Pass. At right is Mike Heney, builder of the White Pass & Yukon Route.

Clifford photo

Hislop, chief surveyor. The latter two were working at the time in Colorado for Graves, who was named president of the corporation.

In a cost-saving move, the company decided to construct a narrow, three-foot gauge line, rather than the newly adopted "official" four foot eight and one-half inch standard gauge, and to use 56-pound rail. Such had been used successfully in construction of railroads in the rugged mountains of Colorado. The narrow gauge allowed for 10-foot instead of 15-foot roadbed and saved considerable in construction costs as well as equipment and operation expenses.

Supplies were ordered and the first arrived on May 27, 1898. Ground was broken the next day.

In the meantime, negotiations were carried out with Brackett to obtain his wagon road. Although he had more than $185,000 invested in the project, Brackett realized that his project was doomed with the Pacific & Arctic Railway obtaining the only right-of-way permit for a railroad from the U.S. Government. He signed an agreement to accept $50,000 as compensation for any damage or losses suffered because of construction of the railroad from Skagway to White Pass, as it was planned that the road would be kept open during construction of the railroad. He also gave the railroad an option to purchase his "toll road and all its franchises, appurtanances and rights," as well as those of the American & Canadian Transportation Co., at any time before July 1, 1899, upon the payment of an additional $50,000.

Five surveying parties took to the hills and vanished for weeks, and in the end turned in five complete surveys covering both sides of the Skagway River as far as the summit. The distance as the crow flies was 14 miles from sea level to the White Pass summit. Putting together bits from each of the surveys as to turn out the best possible line, the group came up with practically the same route that Capt. Billy Moore had laid out a decade earlier—roughly the route of the Skagway Trail.

It was unlikely that there was ever a railroad built with so little advance planning. There was no rolling stock, no construction materials, no heavy equipment, and no means of feeding or housing the construction crews. The site was more than 1,000 miles from the nearest possible supply base, and transportation and communications between the two (Skagway and Seattle) was totally undependable.

More than $200,000 was spent for preliminary supplies before a spade of dirt was turned. Large quantities of dynamite and black powder were required to blast a roadbed through the rocky cliffs between Skagway and Lake Bennett, a total of more than 450 tons in all.

Laborers were recruited in Skagway for 30 cents an hour. They were not the ordinary railroad laborers, being mostly those temporarily detained, waiting the arrival of friends or money and glad to have the opportunity to get cheap board and lodging for a dollar a day in the construction camps. Many were college graduates and professional men swept up in the Klondike rush. On one occasion the White Pass company surgeon, Dr. F. B. Whiting, having an operation to perform, sent out on the grade for an assistant. A skilled physician was found among the graders. He came, assisted the surgeon with the operation, and then took up his pick again.

The work was most difficult. Crews would blow down the side of a mountain, covering the Brackett Road below with debris, then climb down, clear the road and return to the railroad right-of-way. It was slow and expensive, but the Brackett Road had to be kept open to facilitate travel for those enroute to and from Lake Bennett and Skagway and the Klondike, as well as to supply construction camps on the grade further ahead.

One of the early problems was negotiating for a right-of-way along the bluff in Skagway. The town continued to delay the

The skeleton of the old log church at Lake Bennett is a constant reminder of the romance and history of the gold rush days of 1898. Lake Bennett, named after James Gordon Bennett of the New York Herald, was the jumping off point for thousands who took their boats, scows and barges—built during the winter months—into the unknown waters of the north to make their way to the Klondike. Bennett is a popular lunch stop on the White Pass & Yukon Route between Skagway and Whitehorse.

Yukon Travel and Information photo

Lying track down Broadway under the light of the "midnight sun." While tracklayers were hard at work laying rails, some of the townspeople were in a meeting nearby formulating ways of preventing the railroad from running down the main street of town. When the meeting broke up it was too late. The track laying was practically completed.

Clifford collection

easement, and finally the railroad obtained a temporary permit to run the tracks down the main street of town until the other right-of-way became available. This brought a stormy protest from a small but determined group of citizens, who scheduled a meeting for the evening of June 14, 1898 to put a stop to such plans at any cost.

The session was long and heated, so much so that those in the meeting hall apparently could not hear what was going on outside. When the session broke up at about 3 a.m. the protestors, much to their surprise and disappointment, found the railroad construction crews had not been idle. Track was being laid the length of Broadway and men with firearms hanging from their hips were tamping ties.

Despite the many protests, and the eventual laying of track along the bluff on a right-of-way obtained from Capt. Moore along with the use of his facilities for the loading and unloading of ships, the tracks through town remained in use until after World War II.

Chapter V

The Duel On The Dock

Samuel H. Graves returned to the East following the decision to recommend construction of the railway and did not return to Skagway until July 2, 1898. As a friendly gesture upon his return he was invited by Soapy Smith to ride with him and other prominent citizens in the Fourth of July parade. Graves refused the invitation although most of the others accepted. Earlier in the year Smith had unsuccessfully volunteered his "Skagway Guards" for service to the country in the Spanish-American War and received a letter from the War Department thanking him for his patriotism.

Four days after the Fourth Soapy was dead, killed by Frank Reid in a shootout on Juneau wharf, one of four wharves along the waterfront. J. D. Stewart, a miner returning from the Klondike, brought out a poke of gold valued from $2,000 to $2,700. Reports show his arriving in Skagway on July 7 and vary from then on. One states that he lost the gold in a card game in Soapy Smith's Parlor. Another, that he lost it in a "scuffle" behind Smith's resort. A published interview with

They left their mark on Skagway. At the left is Jefferson Randolph "Soapy" Smith, probably the most powerful man in Skagway during the gold rush. At the right is Frank Reid, city surveyor and vigilante. The two met in a gun duel on Juneau Wharf which saw both fatally wounded and which brought the military from Dyea to restore order as an aftermath.

Smith photo Denver Public Library. Reid photo Clifford Collection.

family members in Nanaimo, B.C. after Stewart's return, stated that he checked the poke in the safe of the Mondamin Hotel for the night on advice of two strangers with whom he spent the evening hours. The next morning when he went to claim his gold he was told there was nothing there and that "no one here has ever seen you before."

Whatever the story, Stewart kicked up a rumpus in town and a citizen's committee, long inactive, was reorganized with Graves being named chairman. The "Merchant's Committee" as it was called, may have had numerous businessmen in the ranks, but was in Graves' own words, "a vigilante committee, pure and simple."

Demands were made by the committee that Soapy return the poke by 11 p.m. that evening, although there was no proof that he had anything to do with its disappearance. During the day, Frank Reid, one of the vigilantes, had sharp words on the street with Smith, went to his cabin to obtain a revolver and then sought Smith out at his establishment without success.

A "rump" meeting of the committee was called early in the evening at Sylvester Hall and moved to Juneau Wharf without

Graves being present. Reid was one of the guards stationed at the foot of the causeway to keep out intruders and reputedly was the only one armed.

Learning of the meeting and that Reid had been looking for him, Smith got his Winchester rifle and made his way to the wharf where the meeting was being held and he was being accused and tried without benefit of the court.

Reid blocked his way and Smith made a pass with the Winchester barrel at Reid, who grabbed at the rifle, drew his pistol and pulled the trigger, only to have the hammer fall on a faulty cartridge and fail to fire. Then Smith and Reid fired simultaneously, with Smith being killed instantly and Reid going down, mortally wounded.

The meeting in the warehouse broke up immediately and the committee members, seeing Smith's body of the wharf, went on a rampage in an attempt to round up Smith's cronies. So reckless in their search did they become, that Commissioner C. A. Schlbrede found it necessary to call the troops from Dyea to restore order.

Juneau Wharf, center left, at the foot of Runnals Street (now State Street) where Frank Reid and "Soapy" Smith met and had their famous gun duel which resulted in the death of both. The wharf in the near right corner is Moore's Wharf, built by Captain Billy Moore, and is the basis of the cruise ship wharf of today.

University of Washington

Jeff Smith's Parlor (left) on Holly Street on July 4, 1898. Four day's later the controversial figure was to be killed in a shootout with Frank Reid. Those in front are apparently some of Smith's followers awaiting the start of the July 4th parade. Vandals marred or destroyed the many markers that have been set at the grave of Jefferson Randolph Smith in Skagway's God Rush Cemetery. On the right is one believed to be the original marker, now in the possession of Soapy's grandson, Randy, residing in California.

University of Alaska, Rasmussen collection; Clifford photo

In his book, "On the White Pass Payroll" published in 1908, Graves quotes from a report reputedly made to his superiors dated July 11, 1898, "Reid's death has made the feeling very bitter and we are at wit's end to guard our prisoners from the fury of the mob." Official reports on Reid's death state that he died on July 20, 1898.

Graves' report also stated that the committee had "no shadow of the law to warrant their (Soapy's followers) imprisonment, and still less for taking money found on them and using it to pay for the stolen gold dust and for a fund to pay the expense of legal prosecutions against those that we have evidence against, and to pay the cost of deporting the others."

Smith was buried without ceremony, six feet outside the pioneer cemetery so as not to "desecrate the hallowed ground." Some days later Reid was laid to rest as a hero in the largest funeral in Skagway's history. A large stone marker was placed over the grave with the inscription, "He gave his life for the honor of Skagway."

Chapter VI

Construction of The Railroad

Work continued unabated on the railroad. At Mile 11 two men were drilling a huge granite rock, weighing an estimated 100 tons. Suddenly the rock tumbled forward and the men were crushed. Contractor Heney checked and found the rock immovable. It was marked with a black cross and today it is a towering monument to all of the 35 men who lost their lives in the building of the White Pass & Yukon Route.

Probably no tunnel in the world was built under more difficult circumstances than the one that penetrates a perpendicular rock barrier at Mile 15. Machinery and equipment to drive this 250-foot tunnel were man-handled up the sides of the sheer cliff. When some of the workers refused to take the risk, Heney gave them a choice—do the job or get fired, and then grabbed a rope and equipment and lead the way over the face of the cliff.

Key personnel in the building of the White Pass & Yukon Route in front of the foreman's tent as they take a break from workday chores. Left to right: Mr. Foy, foreman at Construction Camp No. 3; Dr. F.P. Whiting, railroad surgeon; Mike Heney, contractor; E.C. Hawkins, engineer; Samuel H. Graves, president of the White Pass and representative of the British money interests who financed the project; and John Hislop, chief surveyor.

British Columbia Provincial Archives

At the gorge, high on the mountainside overlooking White Pass City, a blast which was described as one "that would put Mt. Vesuvius to shame" was touched off on January 14, 1899. Twenty-seven hundred pounds of dynamite sent tons of rock crashing down the side of the mountain—a blast that could be seen and felt as far away as Skagway.

Graves took special pains in his book to mention the bears in the mountains. At first they ran away and hid from the gold seekers, but later became friendly with humans when the various White Pass survey crews came through with such tasty canned goods as honey, jam, canned milk and the like, which bears were able to snitch from the camps.

Then came the grading crews with their "god-awful" blasting which scared the bears nearly to death and then pelted them with rocks from the sky. They learned quickly, however, that the White Pass crews were not really after them at all—and blasting became a blessing in disguise once they learned about the warnings. They, like the workers, took cover, but once the blast was over made a wild dash—outrunning the workers to their nearby lunch buckets.

Although there were various and sundry disruptions during construction, there were only two major work stoppages.

One was a general strike. During the winter months the company cut back in the number of hours per day worked by the construction crews, but raised the hourly pay to the extent that no worker made less than he did during the summer months. The next spring, when the days once again allowed for longer work hours, the work day was extended and the hourly pay cut back to the old standard. Workers went out on strike and resorted to violence and destruction of property. It was necessary to call out the troops from Dyea to restore order.

On August 8, 1898 and for several days thereafter most of the workers on the road picked up their pay checks and the railroad's picks and shovels and headed off to the Fan Tan

The White Pass & Yukon's first locomotive arrived in Skagway on July 20, 1898 and on the very next day pulled the first train out of Skagway, four miles up the trail towards the summit of White Pass.

University of Washington, Northwest collection

Trail gold strike near Atlin B.C. The work force dropped from 2,000 to less than 700. Few, if any, made as much mining gold as they lost working on the railroad and most were back within a few weeks seeking their old jobs.

Another incident of sorts occurred with the sinking of a train with all hands on board—but no loss of life. It had been the practice to fill in between the precipitous rock points or capes jutting out into Lake Bennett, thus making for a straighter line for track laying. One of the largest such embankments had settled and appeared perfectly solid even after the track was laid and heavy work trains began to rumble over it.

One day, when a work train was crossing, part of the fill suddenly sank under water, taking the entire train except for the engine and a couple of cars. Most of the crew, fortunately, were riding in the engine and only one man went down with the train.

Being a "typical White Pass man," he calmly swam to shore, shook himself and muttered, "Well, I'll be damned!" All the cars except one were recovered.

Construction on the railroad started on May 27, 1898 and by July 21 it was carrying passengers four miles out of Skagway—headed up the canyon toward the goldfields of the Klondike. The rails reached the summit of White Pass on February 20, 1899, and reached the shores of Lake Bennett on July 6, 1899. From then on construction became easier and work started southward from Whitehorse to meet at Carcross (formerly Caribou Crossing) on July 29, 1900 for a gala "Golden" Spike ceremony—just as Dawson City completed its hour on the stage of history and the gold rush began to wane.

Mike Heney's original contract called for the construction to be completed to Lake Bennett in two years. Instead within 27 months he built the entire 110 miles.

Today that railroad construction project remains as a living legend of the past.

Following the "Golden" Spike ceremony, one major project remained. To get the railroad across the chasms at the upper reaches of Dead Horse Gulch another "unsurmountable problem" had been temporarily solved by the use of an ingenious switchback. The train would proceed up the south bank of the canyon to its end, a switch was thrown, and the train backed up across a trestle along the north bank. At this

Construction of the White Pass & Yukon was carried out under the most difficult of conditions. There were no power tools such as in use today. At the left a crude hoist is used to move rocks, loosened by black powder, picks and shovels. At the right workers hang literally "by their teeth" as they chip away at the rock walls at Fisk Cut on Tunnel Mountain in 1898.

point the cars were uncoupled from the engine, the engine was turned around on a covered turntable and coupled up again to the cars. When the train—cars leading and pushed by the locomotive—reached White Pass summit, the engine was cut off and ran around on the siding to its proper location at the head of the train.

Although only a temporary arrangement, much was lost in turning the trains around. With the railroad fully operational at last, construction commenced on a steel arch cantilever bridge spanning the gorge and thus eliminating the switchback. The bridge stood 215 feet above the floor—the highest steel cantilever bridge in the world at the time.

The bridge, although still standing, was replaced in 1969 by a shorter one coupled with a second tunnel through the rocky mountainside.

Construction work continued on the White Pass & Yukon during the sub-zero months and despite winter storms. Bridge workers are seen setting timbers during a blizzard at Tunnel Mountain.

University of Washington, Northwest collection

Impressive ceremonies on July 6, 1899 at Lake Bennett marked the driving of the last spike completing the railroad to this point. Standing in the background are lake steamers awaiting the first load of rail passengers on the way to Whitehorse and Dawson City.

University of Washington, Northwest collection

From sea level at Skagway the WP&YR climbs to 2,885 feet at White Pass summit in only 20 miles of track, one of the steepest railroads in the world. The highest point along the route is at Log Cabin, an elevation of 2,916 feet. Of the 110.7 miles of track, 20.4 miles is in Alaska; 32.2 miles in British Columbia; and 58.1 miles in the Yukon.

The average grade is 2.6 percent with the maximum 4 percent. Approximately 35,000 men worked on the road with 2,000 being the most at any one time. Only 35 deaths occurred, including those who died from disease.

Total cost of the project was approximately $10,000,000.

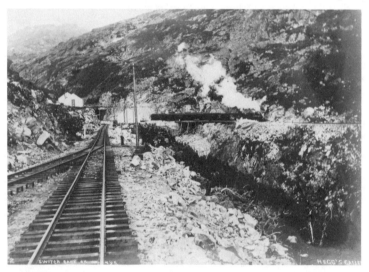

A switchback at the head of Dead Horse Gulch enabled WP&YR trains to get from one side of the deep chasm to the other. The switchback was later replace by a bridge 215 feet above the gulch, the highest cantilever bridge in the world at the time.

University of Washington, Hegg collection

A roundhouse on the far side of Dead Horse Gulch enabled the turning around of the locomotive, which later moved from the rear to the front of the train by means of a siding, thus keeping the engine at the head of the train. The procedure was reversed on the southbound run from Whitehorse to Skagway.

Clifford collection

WHITE PASS & YUKON ROUTE

Chapter VII

Problems Continue

When the rail line was completed to Whitehorse, White Pass officials expected that their troubles would be over and that the dollars would start rolling in. Such, however, was not the case.

Passengers and cargo were being booked through from Skagway to Dawson City, but irresponsible river steamboat operators, competing for business like cab-drivers in front of an ill-managed railroad station, resulted in passengers being fought over, goods stolen on the boats, and through shipments being split up. Near anarchy prevailed.

The railroad formed a river division, the British Yukon Navigation Co., purchasing at the same time the John Irving Navigation Co., which served the Atlin-Lake Bennett region, and included the colorful little Atlin Southern Railway— known as the Taku Tram; and the Canadian Development Co., which operated a winter stage line from Whitehorse to Dawson City and had several sternwheelers on the river.

The first passenger train to make its way from Skagway to Lake Bennett was on July 6, 1899. It was loaded with stampeders heading to the Klondike and on the return trip to Skagway carried a load of successful miners and more than $500,000 in gold from the Klondike.

University of Washington

The first White Pass & Yukon train enroute to the summit of White Pass on February 20, 1899 crosses the East Fork of the Skagway River on one of the many bridges constructed to carry the rails over streams and rivers.

University of Washington, Northwest collection

With the purchase of the Irving properties came the Yukoner, one of the most colorful boats on the river and its most flamboyant captain, Captain John Irving. The vessel was built in Victoria B.C., disassembled for shipment north aboard an ocean-going steamship, and reassembled at St. Michael where the colorful captain selected a popular blonde dancehall girl to do the christening.

The maiden voyage maintained this gay atmosphere. Somehow a crowd of about 300 passengers, musicians, actors, dance hall girls, gamblers and an ample cargo of liquor was packed aboard. As Capt. Irving disliked routine, the Yukoner's first passage up-river was lively and entertaining. With the band playing and the dance hall girls swirling around the deck the captain would approach the docks and landings at ports-of-

Locomotives and freight cars at Lake Bennett as sternwheelers Clifford Sifton, S.C. Bailey and Gleanor prepare to take on freight during the summer of 1899.

Yukon Archives, MacBride Museum collection.

Still carrying the White Pass & Yukon markings and number, open observation coach No. 232 is the only passenger car on the Atlin Southern—also known as the Taku Tram. The former WP&YR locomotive "Duchess" also saw service on this short line across the isthmus from Taku Arm to Scotia Bay. The little railroad was acquired by the White Pass when it took over the assets of the John Irving Transportation Co.

Canadian Pacific Archives

call with throttle wide open, the paddlewheel churning white foam, and the whistle shreiking. Just as disaster seemed imminent, Capt. Irving would go full astern and slide majestically to a stop. Occasionally he misjudged, but that was part of the fun.

A special type of boat was needed on the Whitehorse-Dawson City run as it was necessry to carry heavy loads downstream on a light draft and come back empty against the stream. It was essential that the vessel have enormous backing power with a paddlewheel design sufficiently emerged to take up the power of the engines without racing. The result was a fleet of new White Pass sternwheelers capable of carrying 100 first class passengers and 300 tons of cargo drawing about four feet of water when loaded, and only 18 inches when light. They could steam at about 15 miles an hour and throw a man off his feet when backed suddenly.

The river division initially built three new vessels, the Dawson, Selkirk and Whitehorse and purchased several others.

By 1905 gold had been discovered at Nome and Fairbanks and many of the individual miners had gone downriver. Although there were others who believed that millions of dollars in gold remained in the ground in the Klondike, it would take heavy machinery to recover it. One of the big firms that moved in was Guggenheim Syndicate of New York. Another was headed by "Klondike Joe" Boyle, who had made one fortune in the Dawson area and who later became a hero of international reputation during World War I.

Even in winter tourists wanted to experience the White Pass. This group is pictured at the summit on February 20, 1899, the first such group to make the trip. Note the winter clothing of the day and the many tourists with cameras and tripods.

University of Washington.

Summer tourists started taking trips on the White Pass & Yukon as soon as they became available. This group, organized by the Seattle Post Intelligencer visited Lake Bennett on August 22, 1899. The Seattle paper was one of the first to carry the story of discovery of gold in the Klondike and its readers became extremely interested in the North Country. Today the P.I. still has a large circulation in Alaska.

Yukon Archives

Sternwheelers continued to be the main means of transportation, but scores were now ashore and abandoned. Others died more graphically. The Columbian was destroyed when a crew member decided to shoot ducks from the deck. As he fired his shotgun he stumbled and fired into three tons of blasting powder on the bow.

In 1913 the BYN was engaged in a rate war with Northern Navigation Co., the only U.S. firm on the river. Fares dropped from $26 to $5 for the trip between Whitehorse and Dawson City. The companies eventually "reached and agreement," and in April the White Pass bought Northern Navigation.

In 1923 new competition in the form of the Alaska Railroad came into the picture and additional sternwheelers joined those already decaying along the river. In 1937 there was a resurgence of new mining activity and additional vessels were built, including the Klondike (now on display at Whitehorse). The Keno (now at Dawson City) was refurbished along with other vessels. This was the last major sternwheeler construction project in North America. Population in the Yukon was about 5,000.

With the eruption of World War II, the Alaska Highway project commenced, eventually linking Dawson Creek, B.C. with Whitehorse and Fairbanks. As roads were built the population increased, but use of the sternwheelers declined. Three of the remaining boats were beached in 1951 and the remainder in 1952. The Klondike was given a reprieve a few years later when the White Pass refurbished the vessel to stimulate summer tourist trade, in conjunction with Canadian

690. CLEARING THE TRACK AFTER A SNOW STORM ON THE SUMMIT OF WHITE PASS AND YUKON ROUTE, MAR.20-99

Hundreds of workers were used to clear the track near the summit of White Pass when winter storms hit. This late storm, on March 20, 1899, completely covered the right-of-way.
University of Washington, Northwest collection

Pacific Airlines. The concept was years ahead of its time, and the experiment failed. The Yukon was not ready for tourists or tourists ready for the Yukon.

Concurrent with the starting of steamboat service, the White Pass took over the contracts for winter hauling of both Canadian and U.S. mail and the many sled dog teams involved in the project. The U.S. contract was between Juneau and St. Michael, via Whitehorse with a branch to Nome and several other points. The Canadian portion was between Skagway and Dawson City with a branch to Atlin, B.C.

The WP&YR did not want the winter routes and some 500 dogs but it was necessary for them to assume the year-round responsibility in order to maintain the lucrative summer routes on the river.

Construction of giant dredges, such as this one on Bonanza Creek, resulted in the recovery of additional millions in gold from the Klondike and also resulted in much additional traffic for the White Pass & Yukon railroad in bringing in supplies and construction materials. A similar dredge has been preserved and restored and is on display on Bonanza Creek today.

Clifford collection

In so doing, the White Pass gradually changed from dog teams to horse drawn sledges which carried passengers as well as mail, and even made a little on the winter operation. The company also built roadhouses at intervals along the trail and during the summer months stocked them with supplies for men and horses.

These small hotels of logs provided a warm fire, comfortable beds and good food. Beds were $1.00 a night and meals $1.50. The one-way fare between Dawson City and Whitehorse was $125. Service was cancelled if the temperature fell below minus 40 degrees.

The horse-drawn vehicles remained in service until 1921. Some of the roadhouses, with modern improvements, are still in operation along the highway today.

The White Pass & Yukon sternwheeler Whitehorse makes its way upriver from Dawson City pushing an empty barge enroute back to Whitehorse. The sternwheelers and barges were loaded to the gunwales on the downstream trips.

Yukon Archives

Chapter VIII

Good Years and Bad

As far as the railroad was concerned, there were good years and there were bad years. At one time the WY&YR paid 60 percent dividends to its stockholders, and stock sold in Chicago at the exceedingly high price of $750 a share. These shares were first offered on the market at $6.50 each with a par value of $10.00.

As business slacked off after the Klondike rush, one of the staff suggested to President S. H. Graves that perhaps they might get some tourists to come up and help increase revenue.

Graves turned to the spokesman and asked caustically, "What in hell would a tourist want to come to this god-forsaken country for?"

Graves hadn't reckoned with today's world tourists.

By 1920 gold production began to fall and continued to drop through the 1930's. The Yukon population declined almost to the vanishing point. There was some mining activity and the communities maintained a reasonable level of business during the summer months. They seemed to vanish during the winter.

Over the years the railroad ran further and further into the red and at times was barely able to pay its bond interest. In

This 18-passenger Curtis Condor was one of several planes operated by the White Pass & Yukon on the Whitehorse-Dawson City run. Competition brought fares down to as low as $5 and the railroad soon got out of the airline business, selling out to Grant McConachie, later president of Canadian Pacific Air.

Yukon Archives

addition to sternwheelers, horses and dogs, the WP&YR went into the petroleum business with tank cars and with the advent of World War II a pipeline between Skagway and Whitehorse.

During the winter months senior officers of the company were forced to work without pay and one company president, Herbert Wheeler, mortgaged his home to raise money to meet the payroll.

In 1934 the White Pass & Yukon started an aviation division with the hiring of Vernon Bookwalter, a veteran bush pilot, to operate the division. They purchased a Loening Keystone Commuter and other aircraft and soon added a 10-passenger Ford Tri-Motor, the largest such aircraft in the Yukon. Service was offered between Whitehorse, Carmacks, Minto, Selkirk, Mayo and Skagway. Other planes were added, but by 1939 competition made operation unprofitable and the airline division was sold to Grant McConachie and his Yukon Southern airline. He later became president of Canadian Pacific Air.

As times were not the best, the White Pass—from 1908 to 1938—did not add a single new locomotive to its roster. It was only because of the unusual loyalty of its employees that the company was able to operate for these long, lean years of the Roaring 20's and Hungry 30's.

By the time the 1940's rolled around the railroad had escalated its service somewhat following the development of lead, silver and zinc mining in the Mayo district. Ore was being shipped via riverboat and rail and out through the port at Skagway.

Two new Baldwin locomotives were added in 1939 and two used Alcos were acquired from the Sumpter Valley Railway (Oregon) in 1940. These new arrivals, plus several original White Pass locomotives with more than 30 years service, brought the total of operating engines to eight as World War II burst upon the scene.

The Japanese attack and eventual occupation of the Aleutians graphically showed the importance of an all-weather interior supply route to the North. The answer was the Alaska-Canadian Military Highway (Alcan) which was approved in early spring of 1941. Construction started by March of that same year.

Not only was the White Pass crucial to supply construction of the highway, but it was also called upon to haul equipment for the expansion and development of military airfields and for the immense Canol project—the construction of 640 miles of wilderness pipeline to bring petroleum from the Normal Wells oil fields on the Mackenzie River to the military bases of the North Pacific war.

The White Pass & Yukon was ill-prepared for demands to be made on the little narrow gauge line.

At that time the normal traffic over the line was 12,000 tons annually, with a maximum of two trains a week during the winter months. The initial military need was 1,000 tons a day on a year-round basis, in addition to moving more than 22,000 construction workers and military personnel into the interior.

Try as they could, there was no possible way for the limited

During the winter, travel between Whitehorse, the "end of steel" for the White Pass, and Dawson City was by sledges. Passengers bundled up in furs and the sledges stopped enroute at various roundhouses between the two cities for meals and overnight accommodations. Service was discontinued when the temperature reached minus 40 degrees.

Yukon Archives

Sightseers view Dead Horse Gulch as a passenger train crosses the steel cantilever bridge over the chasm in 1901. The bridge was the highest such structure in the world at the time. Note the "cracks" in the glass negative from which this print was made.

Yukon Archives, H.C. Barley collection

number of White Pass personnel using worn out equipment and a deteriorating roadbed to take on such a project. Much to their credit they did move 67,496 tons in nine months. However, to expedite movement of wartime material, the military leased the operation beginning October 1, 1942 for the duration plus one year.

The arrival of all this cargo and personnel in Whitehorse not only meant that the Alcan Highway was completed ahead of schedule, but also that new runways and hangars could be added to the vital airports along the road. In a feat deemed impossible under the circumstances, the highway started in March 1942 was completed and opened to traffic November 15 that same year.

Ten thousand soldiers divided into seven Army engineer

An early-day White Pass & Yukon locomotive at the railroad shops at Skagway in 1899. Skagway still remains a major work terminal for the railroad today.

Yukon Archives

regiments and 6,000 civilians under the direction of the Public
Roads Administration had completed the job in a single
season—slightly more than six months. They pushed forward
at a rate of eight miles a day, bridged 200 streams, laid a
roadway 26 feet wide between the ditches, and at the highest
point, between Fort Nelson and Watson Lake, reached an
altitude of 4,212 feet.

White Pass & Yukon locomotive No. 5, built for the Columbia and
Puget Sound, was obtained in 1898 and later saw service on the
Klondike Mines Railway. It is on display at Minto Park in Dawson City.
Clifford collection

An early-day White Pass & Yukon train crosses one of the many trestles encountered enroute to the Lake Bennett area. Coach No. 200 and a baggage car complete the train. Many of the early day coaches are still in service on the WP&YR

University of Washington, Northwest collection

The crew of the WP&YR's first snowplow take a welcome break after battling the snow drifts at the summit of White Pass. Today bulldozers are used to combat the snow and ice in the mountains. This snowplow is on display, along with other equipment at Lake Bennett.

University of Washington Library, Northwest collection.

Chapter IX

Whitehorse Is "Discovered"

The construction of the Alcan along with the airports, refineries, etc., brought Whitehorse to the front as a transportation hub. Whitehorse dates back to the Klondike gold rush, but almost 50 years passed before the place "amounted to much," as old-timers say.

The geological formation in the Whitehorse area was responsible for the birth of the city. Miles Canyon, a roaring 3/4-mile-long chasm with walls of basalt 100 feet high was the biggest obstacle on the Yukon River enroute to the Klondike. The treacherous rapids, which someone thought resembled "the manes of white horses," made it a stopping or rest place during the rush. The name had been known for at least 15 years before the rush, although the early history of Whitehorse is vague as nobody paid much attention to the area once they were through the rapids.

During the height of the stampede Norman D. Macaulay and others built wooden tramlines to bypass the canyon and the rapids. The horse-drawn trams were along the east bank of the river and wound up collecting the few cabins that became the start of the city.

A group of stampeders with a horse-drawn tram carrying boat and supplies over one of the tramways in the Whitehorse area. The trams carried supplies around the Miles Canyon and treacherous Whitehorse Rapids. Such was a mark of affluence, not cowardice. Note dog on top of boat and the fact that two of the group, probably the tram operators, have hats with mosquito netting.

Yukon Archives.

Whitehorse was the "end of rail" for the White Pass & Yukon and the "jumping off" place for steamers heading for the Klondike. The river boats operated during the summer months and were stored ashore during the winter when the river was frozen.

Yukon Archives

Then the White Pass & Yukon Railway arrived and although chartered to go through to Fort Selkirk, construcion stopped at Whitehorse as the river was navigable from that point on. The "end of steel," however, was on the west bank of the river, so the town moved across to the railroad. Almost 50 years later Whitehorse had grown to the point that it had spread once again to the east bank.

Whitehorse played second fiddle to Dawson City as the major metropolis of the Yukon until World War II and construction of the Alcan Highway. Road construction lasted only a few months, but the boom continued. By 1955 the riverboats had been replaced by highway travel which branched out from Whitehorse, and the last of the sternwheelers was taken out of service. Centers of activity moved from the river to the highway and southern Yukon began to take on more importance.

The second locomotive on the White Pass & Yukon, along with one of the early-day sledges used on the winter run between Whitehorse and Dawson City, are on display at the MacBride Museum in Whitehorse. The locomotive, a Brooks 2-6-0, was built in 1881 and acquired by the White Pass in 1898.

Clifford photo.

In 1950 Whitehorse was incorporated as a city. Three years later it replaced Dawson City as capital of the Yukon and center of government.

Before highway construction started, Whitehorse had about 300 permanent residents with another 200 coming in for the summer season. Today the population is about 15,000—a far cry from the Whitehorse of the gold rush, which miners referred to as "Just a place to wash your socks."

Passengers and friends awaiting the arrival of a WP&YR train at the Whitehorse depot.

Yukon Travel and Information

Chapter X

The War Years

The first contingent of the 770th Railway Operating Battalion under Lt. Col. William P. Wilson, a veteran of the Burlington operation in the Rockies, moved to the White Pass railroad just as the fiercest northern winter in several decades broke upon the scene.

Temperatures at Whitehorse dropped to 68 degrees below, locomotives in the yards froze to the rails, frost congealed on firebox doors, and drifts continually plugged the line. Even anti-freeze froze in the cans.

On one occasion near Fraser Loop, Col. Wilson and 22 GI's were stranded by drifts with a two-engine train. They shoveled snow into the engine tenders when the water tank froze and burned wooden ties to keep the engine fires alive. Finally it was necessary to move from the train to a small railroad cabin with one stove, designed to house six persons. All attempts to reach them with other rail equipment failed. The desperate situation was relieved somewhat only after a bulldozer ran the length of Lake Bennett on the ice, battling mammoth drifts to get to the isolated cabin with emergency food supplies. After 11 long days they were rescued when a locomotive and rotary snowplow finally broke through from Skagway.

The military started moving in a hodge-podge of equipment. Traffic increased by leaps and bounds until one day they shoved through 34 trains with 2,085 tons on the little single-line railroad.

The army requisitioned additional locomotives from narrow gauge lines throughout the United States and Canada. Narrow gauge cars, many in terrible state of disrepair, were hurriedly diverted north for the WP&YR. Later in 1943 the government sent 10 USRA Baldwins originally destined for Iran to

Jitneys line up to whisk WP&YR passengers arriving at Skagway to nearby hotels or steamships at the dock. The photo was taken before the Golden North Hotel was moved to its present location at Third & Broadway. The Pioneer Hall is in the background.

Yukon Archives

The WP&YR played an important role in the construction of the Alcan Highway during the early days of World War II. Military equipment was landed at Skagway and transported to the Yukon via rail. A train loaded with trucks and other construction equipment heads out from the depot. The dome of the Golden North Hotel is seen in the upper left hand corner.

Clifford collection

Skagway, where they were quickly converted and modified from meter gauge to the 36-inch narrow gauge of the WP&YR.

The special army engines were nicknamed "Gyspy Rose Lees" because they were "stripped for action." One of these locomotives, No. 195, is on display beside the Trail of '98 Museum in Skagway as a reminder of the service rendered by the military during World War II.

At the time the government took over, the railroad was operating 10 locomotives and 38 freight cars. The military added 26 locomotives and 253 freight cars.

Half of the parlor (passenger) cars were commandeered and benches installed to carry personnel. The other half were emptied of their chairs and used to house the men. The chairs became the office equipment for many months at the far north headquarters of Gen. James A. (Patsy) O'Connor of the Northern Service Command.

Not all was peaches and cream. Once a train derailed on the steel bridge spanning a mountain torrent 215 feet below. The soldiers worked with one leg hanging over thin air, but the most serious injury was a lacerated finger. On another occasion, a bulky piece of machinery for the new oil refinery at Whitehorse refused to go around a hairpin curve. The G. I. railroaders chipped away a portion of the cliff and proceeded merrily on their way.

During the last three months of 1942 the railroad moved 25,756 tons of material. In 1942 after the arrival of new equipment and under military operation, the WP&YR moved 281,962 tons—equal to 10 years of pre-war freight. From January 1, 1942 until April 30, 1946, a total of 564,446 tons was handled with the biggest month being August 1943 when 46,606 tons went over the pass. At one time the number of military personnel working on the railroad totaled 600 men.

The soldiers of the 770th—who worked side by side with the White Pass civilian railroaders—became part of the legends of the North. The stories of their experiences "on the toughest 110 miles of track in the world" spread around the globe.

White Pass & Yukon Baldwin No. 195 built for the U.S. Army Corps of Engineers for use in Iran, but diverted to the White Pass and converted to narrow gauge for wartime use. The locomotive is on display between the Trail of '98 Museum and the old Pullen House in Skagway.

Clifford photo

Chapter XI

Post War Years

When the railroad was turned back to civilian management on May 1, 1946 it looked as if the end was near. The military left the line in as bad condition as it was when they took over. Heavy tonnage and endless wear had taken their toll.

The equipment was worn out, business was at a low peak, and all that remained was old and inefficient. Employees, long past their prime as workers remained on the payroll long after they should have been retired—as there was no retirement plan.

The company became unpopular in both Skagway and Whitehorse. Damage claims on shipments ran high. Delayed shipments were blamed on the railroad whether it was responsible or not. The White Pass became the scapegoat for just about everything that went wrong.

The railroad was also in dire need of additional motive

power. The 70 class Baldwins, which had been so successful, were the choice and two more were ordered from the Baldwin works, arriving in 1947 sans tenders.

A few years later additional steam locomotives were required, but no company would re-tool for an order as small as the White Pass had to place. Hence the change to diesels, with the first, Nos. 90 and 91, arriving from General Electric in 1954. As additional diesels came into service the last of the steamers was retired in June 1964, with No. 73 doing the honors on a tourist train.

Most of the old steam equipment was disposed of to tourist railroads in the lower 48, with Nos. 72 and 73 being kept by the White Pass. The former was destroyed in a round house fire on October 19, 1969. Fortunately No. 73 had been moved to Lake Bennett where it was on display with a snowplow and other equipment.

As it became necessary to scrap most of the equipment used by the military and that which was serviceable was upgraded, there was still trouble with breakages, shortages and general

A history of transportation in the Yukon on display at Carcross. One of the horse drawn wagons used in the back country, the sternwheeler Tutshi which operated in the Nares and Tagish Lakes, and the unique little saddle-tanker locomotive "Duchess" which saw service on both the White Pass & Yukon and the Atlin Southern Railway.

Yukon Travel and Information

The White Pass & Yukon has been in the tourist business for more than three-quarters of a century. Pictured are early-day folders, some dating back as early as 1900.

Clifford collection

Little remained after the roundhouse fire of October 15, 1969 which destroyed the Skagway facility. Two new diesels and a switcher were destroyed in the blaze, although little No. 52 steam locomotive, the first on the railroad, was saved from the flames which destroyed six buidlings.

Anchorage Historical & Fine Arts Museum

Two similar passenger trains—one with steam and the other diesel—at
the cruise ship dock. These photos were taken many years ago, but the
same could be made today with both steam and diesel locomotives
again in service over the White Pass & Yukon.

Dedman Photo Shop

disorder in the freight department. It was then that President Frank H. Brown, in a meeting with company officials, conceived the idea of shipping freight from Vancouver in sealed boxes or containers. Thus he set the fuse of what since has become a world-wide container explosion.

In 1951 a new company, the White Pass and Yukon Corporation, was formed. The next few years were ones of growth and modernization. Container ships were built—the 4,000-ton MV Clifford J. Rogers was the first such vessel in the world and served the company for more than a decade before being disposed of and later lost in the Bermuda Triangle.

With the experience gained with the Rogers, two 6,000-ton container vessels, the MV Frank H. Brown and the MV Klondike came into service in the late 1960's and are still owned by the company.

In 1974 Federal Industries purchased a majority of the shares of stock of the White Pass & Yukon Corp. from Ammercosa Investments Ltd., a subsidiary of Angelo American Corp. of Canada Ltd. Federal Industries later obtained all of the stock of the White Pass & Yukon Corp. Ltd.

In the late 1970's, in an effort to perpetuate steam on the historic White Pass, President and Chief Executive Officer Thomas King decided to restore No. 73 and put it back in operation. The locomotive was removed from storage at Lake Bennett and taken to Whitehorse where the tedious work of making her "better than new" was started.

The restoration was successful and the grand old lady had her coming out party—actually two of them—on May 29, 1982 for the Yukon out of Whitehorse, and on June 12 for the southern end of the line out of Skagway. The locomotive operated on a regular schedule during the summer months and was used for charter trips on occasion.

White Pass coaches are still the colorful old passenger cars of a bygone era modernized with oil stoves, thus eliminating the big arguments as to who would stoke the stove during winter runs when the temperatures settle around 30 to 40 degrees below stage.

Although it has never owned a dining car, the WP&YR is probably the best feeder in America as far as railroads go. All through-trains stop at Lake Bennett where sourdough meals are served to one and all, with apple pie—whether it be breakfast, lunch or dinner.

A WP&YR train on Broadway in the summer of 1900. The dome of the Golden North Hotel, then a two-story structure can be seen just behind the locomotive.

Yukon Archives, Vancouver Public Library collection

Today, in comparison with the pre-war years and even during the hectic days of World War II, the railroad carries more freight and passengers than it ever has before. More than 600,000 tons of freight is carried annually over the single-line route, along with 65,000 passengers a year.

The rolling stock on the route is a reflection of the company's ability to respond to user demands. It includes no fewer than 23 diesel-electric locomotives, with four new ones acquired in 1983, 106 container flat cars, 37 tank cars, 4 drop-center flats, 18 dump cars, 3 cabooses, 2 baggage cars and 34 passenger coaches.

The White Pass & Yukon is more than a railroad. The company has become a corporation of major stature. The White Pass & Yukon Corporation Ltd. is a group of wholly-owned and inter-related companies including the three original companies, the Pacific and Arctic Railway and Navigation Co., the British Yukon Railway Co., and the British Columbia Railway Co., along with White Pass Transportation Ltd., Skagway Terminal Co. Pacific and Arctic Pipelines Inc., and

Yukon Pipelines Ltd., whose activities touch many different aspects from the Arctic Ocean to the 49th Parallel...in the Yukon, the Northwest Territories, British Columbia, Alberta and Alaska.

Through these companies the White Pass operates a complex multi-model transportation system via road, rail, ocean and pipeline, spanning international boundaries and covering thousands of route miles.

The White Pass Marine Division originated containerization in 1955 with custom built celluar container-tanker vessels. The division's southern terminal is in North Vancouver and its northern end is the bulk terminal at Skagway.

In more than 35 years of operation the Highway Division has become a leader in northern highway and off-highway transportation. There is also a Highway General Freight Division which serves Alberta, British Columbia, the Yukon and Northwest Territories with schedule and non-scheduled operation. The Petroleum Division not only operates tanker trucks, but also a 4-inch gas-oil pipeline along the rail route to

A modern-day diesel train "poses" for this photo along the shores of Lake Bennett. The WP&YR is a pleasant mix of the old and the new into one of the most interesting and spectacular train trips in North America.

WP&YR photo

Points of Interest On The White Pass Railway

(Numbers represent miles from Skagway)

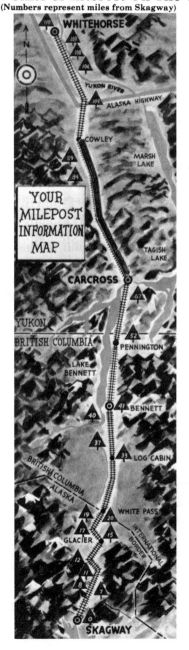

110   Whitehorse. A population of about 12,000—capital of the Yukon, a busy thriving city and located where Alaska Highway and the White Pass Railway meet.

106   To the east is Miles Canyon where Jack London earned his living piloting outfits through the boiling white waters of the Yukon.

67   Carcross. Famous old town on the Trail of '98.

41   Lake Bennett. Old sourdough stopping place where boats were built to float down the Yukon to the Klondike.

40   Lake Lindeman. Head of navigation during the gold rush.

37   Beaver. Lake home of many beaver.

33   Log Cabin. Start of the Fan Tan Gold Trail to Atlin. Once a gold rush town.

20   White Pass Summit. Elevation 2,900 feet, International Boundary.

19   Dead Horse Gulch. Named for 3,000 pack animals that died here during the gold rush of '98.

17   Inspiration Point. Look South to the Upper reaches of Lynn Canal.

15   Tunnel Mountain. White Pass Railway tunnel 1,000 feet above the floor of the gulch. Magnificent view.

12   Bridal Veil Falls. As many as twenty-two cataracts have been seen tumbling down the gorge.

11   Black Cross Rock. 100-ton granite block buried two men during blasting in 1898.

7   Rocky Point. Magnificent view. Railway crosses. Trail of '98.

0   Skagway. Gateway to the Yukon. Once a city of 15,000 during the gold rush.

Whitehorse and by truck to more than 30 Chevron outlets.

Since the beginning in 1898 until today the WP&YR has provided transportation to meet requirements of every phase of Yukon development—through good times and bad—and has continued to stand as a living tribute to the courage and faith of Michael Heney, who defied man and nature to unite the two great empires of the North, Alaska and the Yukon, with a narrow band of steel.

It stands too, as a tribute to the men who spent their lives in the operation of the 110-mile line, from the days of steam to the present diesels, and back to steam again.

Both passenger and freight service on the WP&YR was suspended in the fall of 1982, following the closing of major mines in the Yukon, coupled with rail labor disputes and the opening four years previous of Klondike Highway 2 between Skagway and Carcross.

Efforts were made by several parties, without success, to reestablish service.

After a lapse of more than five years, the WP&YR resumed passenger service between Skagway and White Pass Summit in May 1988, using steam locomotive No. 73 coupled with diesels, over a portion of the route.

The specially designed ore carriers of the WP&YR are just part of the many different types of vehicles owned and operated by the company in order to provide for the needs of the people of the Yukon.

WP&YR photo

The Frank H. Brown, one of the White Pass & Yukon Route container ships which ply the waters between Vancouver B.C. and Skagway with cargo destined to and from the Yukon.

WP&YR photo.

A WP&YR steam passenger train with restored locomotive No. 73 pauses at Lake Bennett while passengers enjoy the sunshine—and an opportunity to partake in a sourdough lunch.

Clifford photo

Passenger Coaches On the WP&YR

200 No name. WP&YR (1902). Scrapped.

201 No name. WP&YR (1900). Baggage car. Runaway, destroyed 1938.

202 No name. Unknown. Acquired 1898. To Klondike Mines Ry. 1904.

203 Now No. 272 Lake Nisutlin.

204 No name. Unknown. Acquired 1898. Sold to Tanana Mines Ry. 1905.

205 No name. Unknown. Acquired 1898. Destroyed in wreck at MP 36 in 1943.

206 No name. Unknown. Acquired 1898. Sold 1918 to Alaska Engineering Commission for use on Tanana Valley lines.

207 Now No. 270 Lake Kathleen.

208 No name. Unknown. Acquired 1899. Sold to Klondike Mines Ry. 1904 as their No. 202.

At the turn of the century the WP&YR on occasion used flat cars with benches and built-up sides and roof to carry sightseeing passengers during the summer months.

Clifford collection

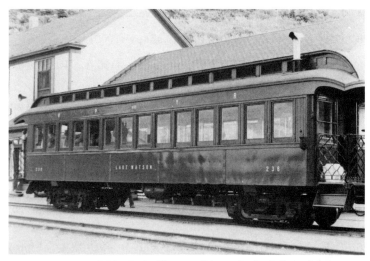

Passenger car No. 238 "Lake Watson" is typical of the unique cars on the White Pass and Yukon Route. This one was one of several built in 1922 in the Skagway shops.

Clifford photo

209   Lake Portage. American Car & Foundry (1918). Ex-Sumpter Valley Ry. Combination car.

210   No name. Unknown. Acquired 1899. Sold 1905 to Tanana Mines Ry. as their No. 100.

211   No name. American Car & Foundry (1918). Ex-Sumpter Valley Ry. Last side-door combination car on WP&YR.

212   No name. Unknown. Acquired 1899. Destroyed in roundhouse fire in 1932.

214   No name. Unknown. Acquired in 1899. Combination car.

216   No name. Unknown. Acquired in 1899. Sister car to No. 214. Possibly from Philippines or Coeur d'Alene Railway & Navigation Co. Combination car.

218   Lake Atlin. Unknown. In use on WP&YR in 1900.

220   Lake Dewey. Unknown. Same as No. 218.

222   Lake Lindeman. Unknown. Same as No. 218.

224 Lake Marsh. Unknown. Same as No. 218.

226 Lake Fraser. WP&YR Skagway shops (1903).

228 No name. Built WP&YR Skagway (1903). Destroyed in Skagway roundhouse fire in 1932.

230 No name. WP&YR Skagway (1908). Observation car with open sides. Walled in and used as bunk car during World War II. Destroyed in fire at MP 14 October 1943.

232 No name. WP&YR Skagway (1908). Observation car with open sides. Sold to Atlin Southern "Taku Tram" 1917. Used as bunk car 1942. Scrapped after World War II.

234 Lake Cowley. Unknown. On WP&YR in 1916. Ex-California-Nevada RR.

236 Lake Mayo. Unknown. On WP&YR in 1916. Ex-California-Nevada RR.

238 Lake Watson. WP&YR Skagway shops (1922).

240 Lake Bennett. Unknown. Acquired in 1926. Ex-Arizona RR No. 3.

242 Lake Teslin. Unknown. Acquired in 1927. Ex-Arizona RR No. 7. Originally built for Utah and Northern RR. Believed to be private coach for Brigham Young, famed Morman leader.

244 Lake Emerald. Carter Bros., San Francisco (1883). Ex-Northwestern Pacific No. 731. Acquired in 1927. Possibly oldest car on WP&YR.

246 Now No. 264 Lake Aishihik.

248 Lake Tagish. Carter Bros., San Francisco (1887). Ex-North Pacific Coast No. 728. Acquired in 1938.

250 No name. Pullman Co. (1893). Ex-North Pacific Coast No. 713. Acquired 1930. Destroyed in roundhouse fire 1932.

252 Lake Muncho. Pullman (1893). Ex-Northwestern Pacific No. 716. Acquired in 1930.

254 Lake Dezadeash. Pullman (1893). Ex-Northwestern Pacific No. 717. Acquired in 1934.

256 Lake LeBarge. Pacific Car & Foundry (1936) Acquired new. "Queen's Car." First all-steel car on WP&YR and used on the special train for Queen Elizabeth II and Prince Phillip of Britain on visit to Whitehorse in 1959.

258 Lake Kluane. J. Hammond (1893). Ex-Pacific Coast No. 102. Acquired in 1938.

260 Lake Tutshi. J. Hammond (1893). Ex-Pacific Coast No. 103. Acquired in 1939. Used in 1935 Universal Studios film "Diamond Jim Brady" as steel test car crashed into wooden coach on "New York Central in 1870" to prove safety of all-steel coach design.

262 Lake Summit. J. Hammond (1893). Ex-Pacific Coast No. 105. Acquired 1938. Destroyed in Skagway roundhouse fire 1969.

264 Lake Aishihik. Carter Bros., San Francisco (1884). Ex-North Pacific Coast No. 732. Acquired in 1927. Ex-WP&YR No. 246.

266 Lake Schwatka. American Car & Foundry (1918). Ex-Sumpter Valley Ry. Acquired in 1940.

268 Lake Lewes. American Car & Foundry (1918). Ex-Sumpter Valley Ry. Acquired in 1940.

270 Lake Kathleen. J. Hammond (1893). Ex-Pacific Coast Ry. No. 201. Acquired in 1939. Ex-WP&YR No. 207 (baggage car).

272 Lake Nisutlin. WP&YR Skagway shops (1900). Ex-WP&YR No. 203 (baggage car).

274 Lake Primrose. Coast Steel Fabricators Ltd. (1970). Built new for WP&YR.

276 Lake Big Salmon. Same as No. 274

278 Lake Fairweather. Same as No. 274.

280 Lake Dease. Same as No. 274.

282 Lake Klukshu. Coast Steel Fabricators Ltd. (1974). Built new for WP&YR.

284 Lake Takhini. Same as No. 282.

286 Lake Kusawa. Same as No. 282.

288 Lake McClintock. Same as No. 282.

White Pass & Yukon Locomotive Roster

"Georgiana"   0-6-0T Baldwin #3713, April 1875. Seattle & Walla Walla 1878. Sold to WP&YR 1898 but never shown on engine roster. Believed to have been lost with other equipment in shipwreck enroute to Skagway.

"Duchess"   0-6-0T Baldwin #4424, Sept. 1878. Built for Dunsmuir, Diggle & Co. as 2'6" gauge "Duchess." Wellington Colliery Ry. No. 2; WP&Y "Duchess" 1899; Atlin Southern Ry. "Duchess" 1899-1919. Retired and on display at Carcross. When widened to 3¼ gauge in 1899, the first driver was not coupled to the rods, making the engine an 0-(2)4-0T.

No. 1-51   2-6-0 Brooks 1881 Seattle & Walla No. 3; Columbia & Puget Sound No. 3; believed to be Ex-Utah & Northern. To WP&Y 1898. Rebuilt and renumbered No. 51 in 1900. To Atlin Southern 1919 and back to WP&Y in 1931. Retired in 1941 and on display at Whitehorse, Y.T.

No. 2-52   2-6-0 Brooks 1881. Seattle & Walla, No. 4; Columbia & Puget Sound No. 4; believed to be Ex-Utah & Northern. To WP&YR 1898 as first WP&Y locomotive. Arrived in Skagway July 20, 1898. Rebuilt and renumbered No. 52 in 1900. To Atlin Southern 1931, back to WP&Y in 1937. Retired in 1940 and on display at Skagway.

No. 3-53   2-8-0 Grant, 8/1882. Cincinnati & St. Louis No. 63; Dayton & Ironton No. 63, 1884; Columbia & Puget Sound No. 9, 1887. WP&Y 1898. Remodeled and renumbered No. 53 in 1900. Scrapped 1918.

No. 4-54   4-4-0 Baldwin #4294, 3/1878, Olympia & Tenino (later Olympia & Chehalis Valley) No. 1. "Quimette"; Columbia & Puget Sound Sound No. 10, 1890; WP&Y 1898. Rebuilt and renumbered No. 54 in 1900. To Tanana Mines Ry. (Tanana Valley) No. 50, 1905; Alaska Engineering Commission (Alaska Railroad) 1917. Scrapped 1930.

No. 4 (2nd)   2-6-2 Baldwin #37564, 3/1912. Klondike Mines Ry. No. 4 (2nd) 1942. To Oak Creek Central Ry. 1952; Petticoat Junction RR. Sevierville, Tenn., 1965.

This Brooks 2-6-0 locomotive, the first engine on the WP&YR is on display downtown Skagway. The engine, No. 2 and then renumbered No. 52 when rebuilt in 1900, also saw service on the Atlin Southern before being returned to the White Pass and retired in 1940.

Clifford photo.

Three former White Pass & Yukon locomotives which later saw service with the Klondike Mines Railway are on display at Dawson City's Minto Park. They are KM No. 1 Brooks, formerly White Pass No. 63; KM No. 3 Baldwin formerly White Pass Nos. 7 and 57; and KM No. 2 Baldwin former White Pass Nos. 5 and 55; and a former Northern Light, Power, Coal and Transportation No. 4 Porter.

Clifford photo

No. 5-55	2-8-0 Baldwin #7597, 5/1885. Columbia & Puget Sound No. 8. WP&Y 1898. Rebuilt and renumbered No. 55, 1900. To Klondike Mines No. 2, 1904. On display at Dawson City, Y.T.
No. 6-56	2-8-0 Baldwin #16455, 1/1899. First new locomotive on WP&YR. Renumbered in 1900. Rebuilt from Vauclain compound to simple in 1907. Scrapped 1938.
No. 7-57	2-8-0 Baldwin #16456, 1/1899. Renumbered No. 57, 1900. To Klondike Mines Ry. No. 3, 1906. On display in Dawson City Y.T. Last remaining Vauclain compound in Canada.
No. 8-58	3-truck. Climax #167. 12/1897, Columbia & Northwestern No. 2; Pacific Contract Co. (WP&Y) No. 8, 1899; Renumbered No. 58, 1900. Sold to Maytown Lumber Co. 1903. Scrapped.
No. 10	4-6-0 Baldwin #42766, 1/1915 East Tennessee & Western North Carolina No. 10; United States Army Transportation Corps., assigned to WP&Y No. 10 1942-45; Damaged in Whitehorse roundhouse fire Dec. 1943, returned to Seattle and scrapped 12/1945.
No. 14	4-6-0 Baldwin #52406, 9/1919. East Tennessee & Western North Carolina No. 14; USATC No. 14 1942-45. Damaged in Whitehorse roundhouse fire Dec. 1943, returned to Seattle and scrapped 12/1945.
No. 20	2-8-0 Baldwin #11355, 12/1890. Denver, Leadville & Gunnison No. 272; Colorado & Southern No. 69, 1899; USATC No. 20, 1943. Retired 1944 and scrapped in Seattle 12/1945.
No. 21	2-8-0 Baldwin #11356, 1890. Denver, Leadville & Gunnison No. 273; Colorado & Southern No. 70 1899; USATC No. 21, 1943. Scrapped in Seattle 12/1945.
No. 22	2-8-0 Baldwin #24109, 4/1904. Silverton Northern No. 3; USATC No. 22 1943. Retired 1944 and scrapped in Seattle 12/1945.
No. 23	2-8-0 Baldwin #27977, 4/1906. Silverton Northern No. 4; USATC No. 23, 1943. Retired and scrapped in Seattle 12/1945.

No. 24	2-8-0 Baldwin #24130, 12/1904. Silverton Gladstone & Northerly No. 34; Silverton Northern No. 34. 1915; USATC No. 24, 1943-47. Retired 1944 and scrapped in Skagway 1951.
No. 59	4-6-0 Baldwin #17749, 5/1900. Scrapped 1941.
No. 60	4-6-0 Baldwin #17750, 5/1900. Retired 12/1942; used as riprap fill in Skagway River MP 2.5 in 1949.
No. 61	2-8-0 Baldwin #17814, 6/1900. Retired 1944; used as riprap fill Skagway River MP 2.5 in 1949.
No. 62	4-6-0 Baldwin #17895, 6/1900. Retired 1945, used as riprap fill Skagway River MP 2.3 in 1949.
No. 63	2-6-0 Brooks #522, 1881. Kansas Central Ry. No. 102 & No. 7. WP&Y, June 1900. Klondike Mines Ry. No. 1 in 1902. On display at Dawson City, Y.T.
No. 64	2-6-0 Hinkley 1878. Purchased 1900 from Canadian Pacific Railroad. Ex-Columbia & Western (Trail Tramway) No. 2. Scrapped 1918.
No. 65	2-6-0 Brooks #578, 1881. Kansas Central No. 8; Union Pacific No. 102, 1885; Columbia & Western No. 3; Utah & Northern; Columbia & Western (Trail Tramway) No. 3; Canadian Pacific; White Pass & Yukon No. 65. 1900; Tanana Mines (Valley) No. 51, 1906; AEC (Alaska Railroad) No. 51, 1917. Scrapped by Alaska RR 1930.
No. 66	4-6-0 Baldwin #18964, 5/1901. Retired 1953. Cab to No. 69.
No. 67	4-6-0 Baldwin #18965 5/1901. Retired 1941, used as riprap in Skagway River 1951.
No. 68	2-8-0 Baldwin #30998, 6/1907. Destroyed by rock slide at MP 15.6 Aug. 17, 1917.
No. 69	2-8-0 Baldwin #32962, 6/1908. Retired 1954. Sold to Black Hills Central RR No. 69, "Klondike Casey" 1954; Nebraska Northern No. 69.
Nos. 70 & 71	2-8-2 Baldwin #62234-57, 5/1938 and 1/1939. Retired 1963 and stored. Sold to "Whistle in the Woods" Corp. for restoration.

Nos. 72 & 73   2-8-2 Baldwin #73351-52, 5/1947. Retired June 30, 1964 and stored. No. 72 destroyed in roundhouse fire, Skagway, Oct. 15, 1969. No. 73 restored and back in service on WP&YR 1982.

No. 152   4-6-0 Baldwin #53269, 6/20. Alaskan Engineering Commission for Tanana Valley No. 152. Retired in 1932 and stored. To U.S. Army No. 152 for use on WP&YR. To Lathrop Transportation Corps Depot, Calif., 1945; Davidson Scrap Metals Co., Stockton, Calif.; Hal Wilmunder (Antelope & Western Ry. No. 3), Roseville, Calif.; Camino, Cable & Northern, Camino, Calif.; Keystone Locomotive Company 1974; Huckleberry Railroad (Mt. Morris, Minn.) No. 2, 1975.

Nos. 190-200   2-8-2 Baldwin #69425-35 incl. 2/1943. Built for U.S. Army Corps of Engineers as meter-gauge for use in Iran, diverted and converted to 3′ gauge. All USA same numbers.

  190   1943-46, retired 1946. Sold Tweetsie RR No. 190 "Yukon Queen" in 1960.
  191   1943-47, retired 1946, scrapped 1951.
  192   1943-46, retired 1960, sold Rebel RR No. 192 "Klondike Kate" 1961.

Steam locomotive No. 73 heads a passenger train crossing the Glacier Bridge enroute over White Pass to Lake Bennett. The steam trains run on a regular schedule during the summer months.

Clifford photo

193	1943-47, retired 1946, scrapped 1951.
194	1943-47, retired 1946, scrapped 1951.
195	1943-45, retired 1946, on display in Skagway.
196	1943-45, retired 1961, stored unserviceable.
197	1943-47, retired 1944, scrapped 1951.
198	1943-44, scrapped Seattle 1945.
199	1943-44, scrapped Seattle 1945.
200	1943-44, scrapped Seattle 1945.

Nos. 250-256   2-8-2 Alco #64981 —82, —83, —85, —86, —88, —90, 9/1923. Ex-Denver & Rio Grande Western Nos. 470, 471, 472, 474, 475, 477, 479. USA 1942/44 Nos. 250-256. No. 250 scrapped Seattle 1944; 251 Seattle 1945; 252 Ogden 1945, boiler to Pueblo; 253-256, scrapped Seattle 1945.

White Pass & Yukon snowplow No. 2 and an Alco 2-8-2 locomotive are seen while enroute to the Sumpter Valley line in Oregon. The Alco is one of two which came to the White Pass during World War II and then eventually sent back to Oregon after being retired from service.

Clifford photo.

Diesels

| Nos. 90-91 | General Electric #32060-61. 800 hp. June 1954. |
| Nos. 92-94 | General Electric #32709-11. 890 hp. Dec. 1956. |

Nos 95-97	General Electric #34592-94. 890 hp. March 1963. Being scrapped for parts.
Nos. 98-100	General Electric #35790-92. 990 hp. May 1966.
Nos. 101-107	Alco #602302, 03, 04, 06, 07. 1200 hp. 1969.
Nos. 108-110	Alco #605401-03. 1200 hp. 1972.
Nos. 111-114	Bombardier Inc. #61231-34. 1200 hp. 1983.

Switchers

| No. 1 | General Electric #28109. 150 hp. Sold 1969. |
| No. 81 | General Electric #32933. 800 hp. 1957. Ex-U.S. Army. To Guatemala, Bandegur Nos. 314, 20281. |

The White Pass and Yukon Corporation Limited